shame

embrace

palms

blasts leave me

stars

trees

saintagatha
mother
redeemer

michèle saint-michel

Published by Bad Saturn. BAD SATURN and associated
logos are trademarks and/or registered trademarks.

LIBRARY OF CONGRESS
CATALOGING-IN-PUBLICATION DATA
Saint-Michel, Michèle.
Saint Agatha Mother Redeemer / by Michèle Saint-Michel.
– 1st ed.
p.   cm.
ISBN: 978-0-9999020-7-3

Summary: Using the words of dead poets and writers,
this fully-illustrated book of erasure poetry explores the
multi-temporalities of healing after trauma.
Told through layered imagery, text messages, and illustrated
self-portraiture, Saint Agatha Mother Redeemer takes you on
a journey through the unsteady waters of healing after
traumatic events and living with PTSD.

sparkling

ballasts leave me

trees

T niches aside and junior

missing,

A sorbing all to myself ar

It seems to me more than

"We are cut, we are fallen.
We are become part of that unfeeling
universe that sleeps when we are at
our quickest and burns red
when we lie asleep."

– Virginia Woolf

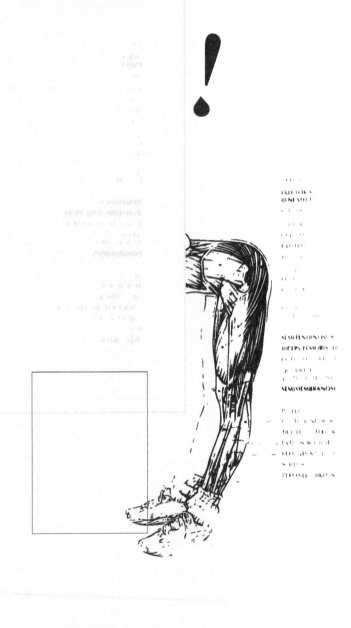

CONTENTS

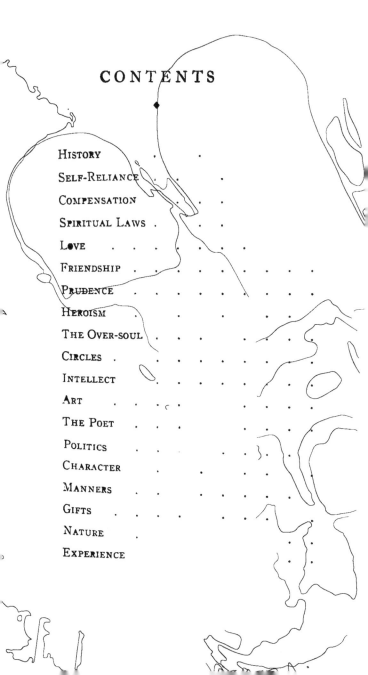

HISTORY

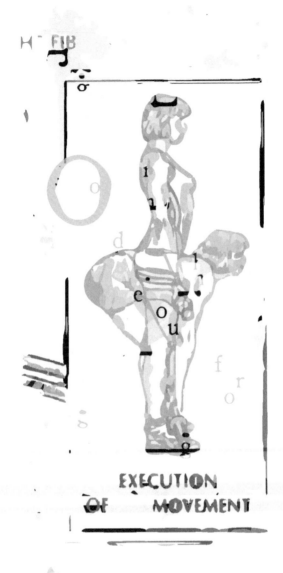

EXECUTION
OF   MOVEMENT

SACRE   OS COXA

They rise together, they
I see in them myself   tl
I believe in those wing'd ⌐
sinewy shapes
And acknowledge, yell
the gentle semi-roar
good enough for a carcas s
when they seest me

Hear to him—hear to me
the muscle; red
the increasing stomach
the gentle semi-roar
coloring with rising fury,
distant and day-long \
would tell a different story.

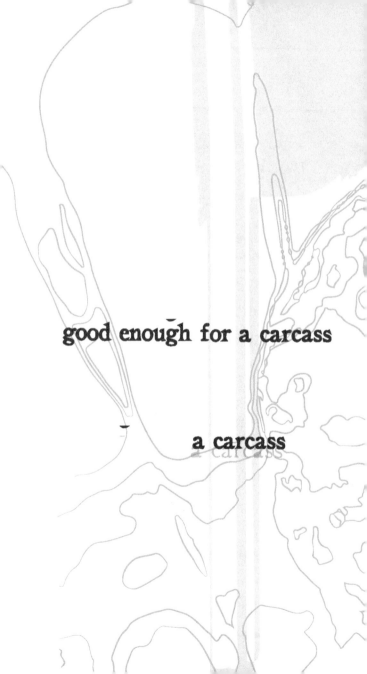

good enough for a carcass

a carcass

good enough for a carcass

o
o

o
o
o
o
o
i

o
i
o
d
l
l
e
o
u
o
f
r
o
o
g

good enough for a carcass
good enough for a carcass
good enough for a carcass
good enough for a carcass
good enough for a carcass

Do you think I could walk pleasantly
and well-suited toward
annihilation?

I could

(What is less or more than a touch?)

Only what nobody denies is so.

I believe a leaf of grass is no less

than the journey-work of

the stars,

the palm crown

the amphitheatre

all to stifle rising fury

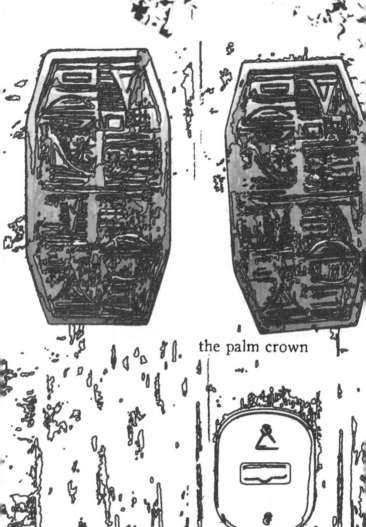

the palm crown

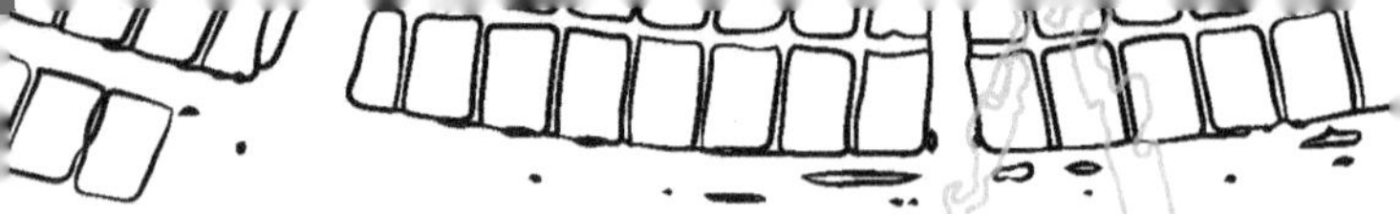

Start with Statement 1

Divinity is the law of right and wrong

Here is the rephrased problem:

there were no clouds
gazing at the bright planet
the Milky Way with its branches
topmost twig of the birch-tree
                edges of Divinity
stitched togethe

                blindness

Swallowed
an ent're mountain range
flash of lightning the Milky Way
whole from my perspective
        an illusion

    I am made one
with other men in one body
                    of believers
the rotation of the earth
over   space obscuring it
        Correctiv strength
the world by revelation

    "But what am I questioning?"

"Don't I know that the stars don't move?"

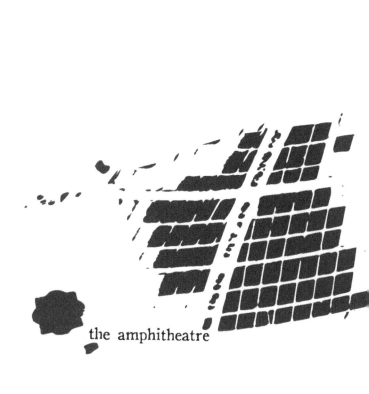

the amphitheatre

"And could the astronomers
have understood and calculated
anything, if they had taken into
account all the complicated and
varied motions of the earth?
All the marvelous conclusions
they have

out, adorned with green dock
appeared as splendidly and s
all those rare and foreign in
them. Then were the gener
mple and sincere expressions i
onceived, without seeking artifi
had fraud, deceit, and malice
. Justice maintained her prop
favor and interest, which now
te her. Law was not ye left
en there was neither cause nor
ore, went about alone, without
dom and lewd designs of other.
ly owing to their own natural i
estable ages of ours and damse
inclosed in another laventh
gh some cranny or through
the colours residence find e
pite of all seclusion. Therefore,
increased, to defend maidens,
ans and persons distressed, th

Spiritual Laws

behold the
picturesque giant

' '
a ' l
l
a '
c c
t
a¹ (c
t
a¹
t
l
'

and stop there,
and stop there,
and stop there,
and stop there
and stop th
and stop
and st

stop

and stop here

ere,
there,

And do
not call'

And do
not call

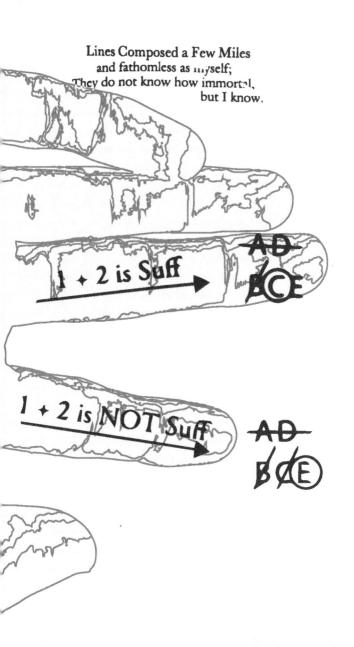

Lines Composed a Few Miles
and fathomless as myself;
They do not know how immortal,
but I know.

1 + 2 is Suff

AD
B C E

1 + 2 is NOT Suff

AD
B C E

And do,
no
t. c
a
ll
the
tortoise

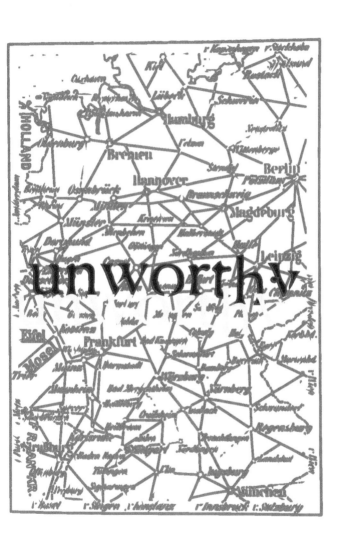

LOVE

and to
foreign in

un
protected

s ‖‖‖‖‖l,

ent un

worthy

Maidens went about alone
without fear of danger
deeply in love above all
for your pleasure and amusement
in these detestable ages of ours
no damsel is secure

unbelievable

hidden and inclosed in another labyrinth like that
there, through some cranny, or through the air,
importunity, the amours pestilence find entrance
r k d   t f ll l   1

reached
the
heavenly
before me
and
just as
uncertai
relation to
conclusions
of right
has been
trusted
to Divinity

Logic
and
sermons
never
convince

fears neither God nor devil,

leagues out of his course to

do a poor devil a service

to that low and feverish murmur

which precedes all great events

FRIENDSHIP

X

wyd?

MESSAGES

A minute and
a drop of me

l

l

l

b

l

l

l

c

l

c

s

r

what is behind me
for good reason
settle my brain

This is the meal

looking at the movements of the
stars, I can't picture to myself
the rotation of the earth.
                        and I'm right

in saying that the stars move
            "A d   ld h

theto•p•mo•s•tw•g•o•f•he•b•irc-h-tre--e

what is behind me
hand, puts to see a
long-threaded moss fruits,

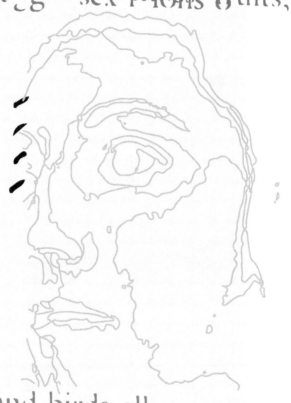

ds, and birds all over,
nd me for good reasons,
I desire it

tell
a
different
story."

PRUDENCE

The kept woman

elegant
cunningly wrought
the circumstances
vary every hour.

a cheerful present
losing in violence
time in either breast
they confess and flee

inventions, conceptions
the same artificial phrases
leaves and sinewy
malice intermixed

left to the
            fear of danger
for good reasons,
    inhabit this temple
of the body

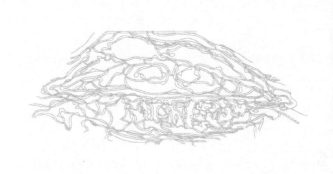

Evaluate ONLY Statement 1

Statement 1

Heyyyyyy

touch
of my
still

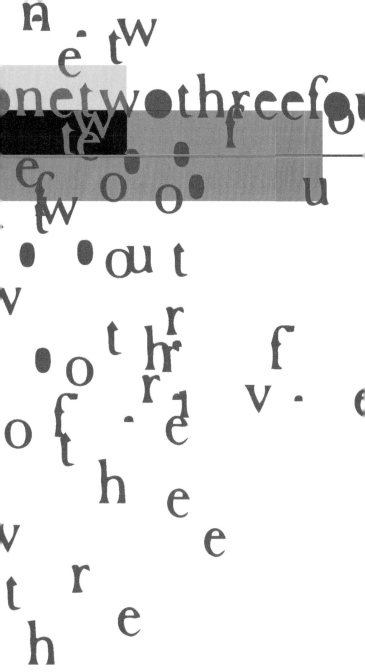

I beat
and
pound
for the
dead

THE C

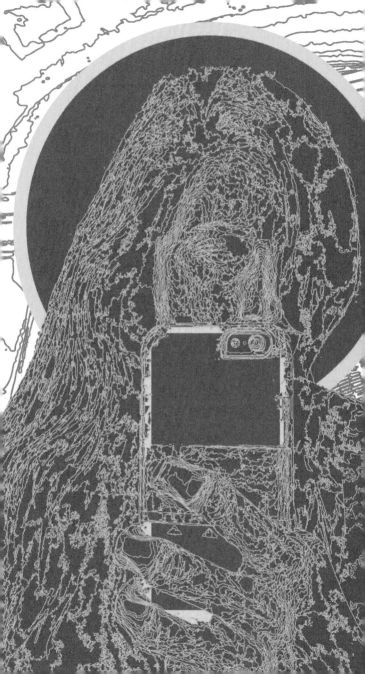

p g   j

he was
a w a s
a hand
some
man

ethat

Jesus

gentle

Did your pain feel steady?

Not at all

Did your pain feel electrical?

A little bit

Not at all   Did your pain feel sore?

Somewhat

A little bit   Not at all

Quite a bit

Somewhat   A little bit

Very much

Quite a bit   Somewhat

Skip question

Very much   Quite a bit   Did your pain feel deep?

Did your pain feel stinging?

Very much

Not at all

Not at all   Did your pain feel numb?

A little bit

A little bit   And acknowledge , yell

Somewhat

Not at all

Somewhat   Quite a bit

Did your pain feel achy?

Very much

Quite a bit   Somewhat

Not at all

Very much   Quite a bit

A little bit

Did your pain feel tingly?

Very much

Somewhat

Not at all

A little bit   Quite a bit

Somewhat   Very much   Did your pain feel like pins and needles?

Did your pain feel tender?

Quite a bit   Not at all

Not at all

Very much

A little bit

A little bit

Somewhat

Somewhat

Quite a bit

Quite a bit

Very much

Very much

Very much

HEROISM

Brief Quest

The following questions ask about events that may be extraordinarily stressful or disturbing for everyone.

Please circle one number, 0-3.

32 Unnecessary or over-fre uent washin

Low sex drive

31 Feelin that thin s are "unreal"

12 Loneliness

1 Dizziness

21 Fear of men

13 Ni htmares

1 Not feelin satisfies with our sex life

3 Passin out

2 Uncontrollable c in

2 Fear of women

1 . Wakin u earl in the mornin

3 Feelin s of uilt

Restless slee

. Sexual feelings when you shouldn't have them

33. Feelin s of inferiont

3 . Desire to physically hurt others

3 Havin trouble breathin

Feelin isolated from others

2 Insomnia

2 . Bad thoughts or feelings during sex

22. Not feelin rested in the mornin

1 Anxie attacks

23 Having sex that you didn't enjoy

11. Sexual overactivit

1 Headaches

2 . Desire to h sicall hurt ourself

2 Wakin u in the middle of the ni ht

1 . Sadness

3 Feeling that you are not always in your body

2 Trouble ettin alon with others

Sexual problems

"Flashbacks" (sudden, vivid, distracting memories) .

3 Feeling tense all the time

Stomach roblems .

3 Bein confused about our sexual feelin s

2 . Memory problems

1 . Trouble controlling your temper

1 . "Spacing out" (going away in your mind)

3 Weight loss (without dieting)

Did your pain feel deep?

Did your pain feel tender?

Very much

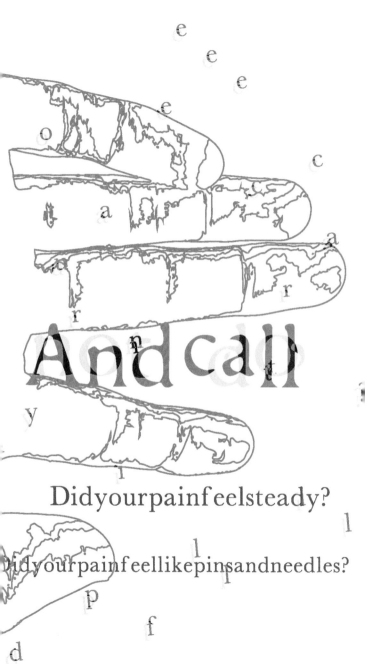

And call

Didyourpainfeelsteady?

Didyourpainfeellikepinsandneedles?

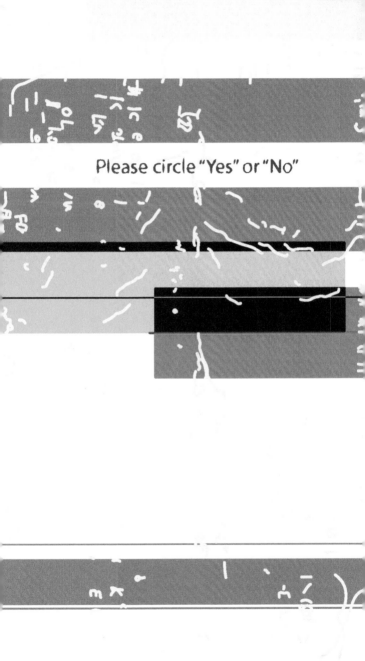

Please circle "Yes" or "No"

1. Have you ever served [in]
   a noncombat job that [for]
   example [as] a medic o

2. Have you ever been in [an]
   accident at work or so

3. Have you ever been in [such]
   such as a fire, tornado,
   spill?

4. Have you ever had a lif[e]
   attack, leukemia, AIDS

5. Before you were yo[u]
   parent, [or] te[ll]
   you thought you wou[ld]
   welts, lumps or other [?]

6. Not including any pun[ishment]
   Question 5, have yo[u]
   anyone, including frien[ds]

7. Has anyone ever made
   unwanted sexual cont[act]

Note: By sexual contact we
else and your private parts
private parts

8. Have you ever been in
   seriously injured, or ha[s]
   which you feared you

9. Has a close family mer[ber]
   a serious car crash, mu[rder]

10. Have you ever witness[ed]
    seriously injured or kil[led]
    in which you feared so

Note: Do not answer "yes"
Questions 1-9

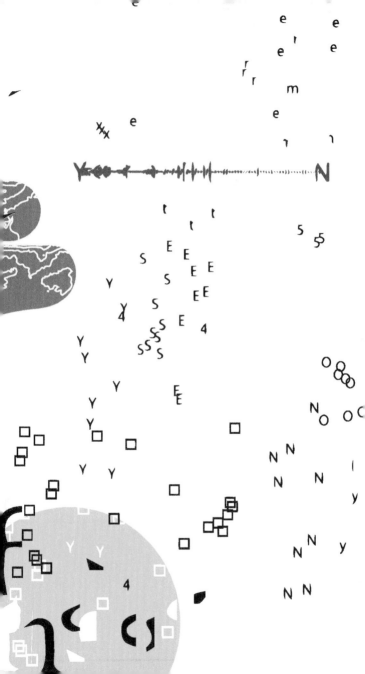

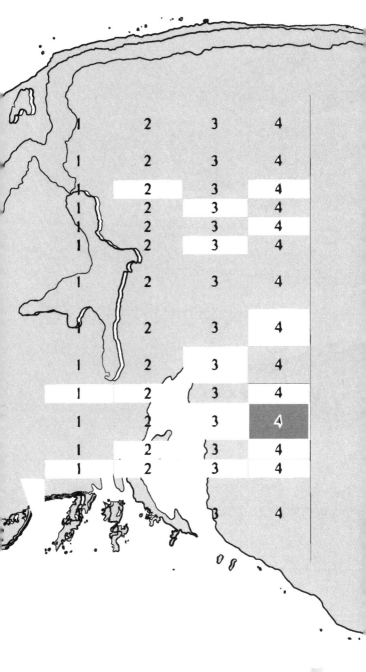

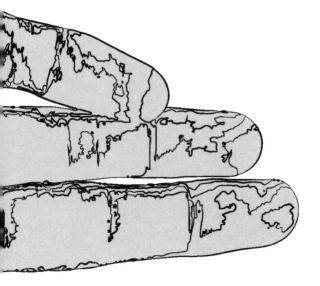

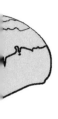

I see in
th em
myself.

1. Have you

2. Have you

3. Have you

4. Have you

5. Before ag

6. Not   u

7. Ha

Note:
   and you
   parts

8. Have you
   seriously

9. Has
   a serious c

10. Have you
    seriously

THE OVER-SOUL

No Yes	No Yes	No Yes
No Yes	No Yes	No Yes
No Yes	No Yes	No Yes
No Yes	No Yes	N/A
No Yes	No Yes	No Yes
No Yes	No Yes	No Yes
No Yes	No Yes	No Yes
No Yes		No Yes
No Yes		No Yes
No Yes		N/A

MESSAGES

I see
them

elt

voided

u t about it

hought   I didn`t mea

felt as if it hadn`t happened or was

sta ed awa from reminders of it.

ictures about it po   ed into m mi

I was jum   and easil startled.

tried not to think about it.

I   as aware that I still had a lot of

lings about it, but I didn`t deal

My feelings about it were numb

I found myself feeling like I

s back at that time.

. I had trouble fallin aslee

. I h d waves of strong feelings

. I tri d to remove it from m mem

. I had trouble concentrating

. Reminders of it caused me to ha

ical reactions such as sweating

You have
memories to
look back on

No   Yes

No   Yes

Chats

 Tap for more info

 You were

New

ee st in
made by circumstances

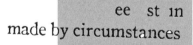

Status

Calls

Camera

Chats

Settings

"Le t us o nly

ta lko f yo ur

h appo yre turn."

That is right and yet

You have 1, 2, 3, 6, 9, 14, 16, 20 missed calls
You have 5, 7, 8, 11, 12, 13, 17, missed calls
You have 4, 10, 15, 18, 19, 21 missed calls

I had tro
I felt
I avoided
I thou   a
I thought
I felt as
real.
I sta ed
Pictures
I was j
tried
I   as a
feelings abo
My fee
I found
was back
I had tr
I h d w
I tri d
I had t
Remin
physical re
trouble br
heart.

CIRCLES

You have
memories to
look back on

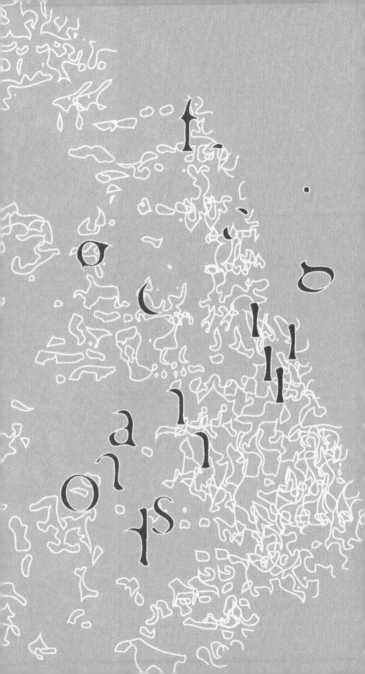

about what was talked about
I need to say

u asked me if I could say with certainty
that risk is 0%

I cannot in good conscious

have to tell

I was caught up in the heat wasn't thinking clearly

mistake
dishonest rep

never

I'm having a hard time
believing   n't safe

convince,

inaction
proof responsibility

That is right and yet

y

the limits of nature give power

tried not to think about it.

letting myself get upset when

physical reactions, such as sweating,
trouble breathing, nausea, or a pounding
heart.

dv ssfion g   f e e nlgs
drtv ext fr   om   mm   eo
dr.l obon   t ra tin g
ind éfi n as   e d m   eo   ha e
r s?nth   as   s we an g .
rb antgue   a,   o r pe un ic

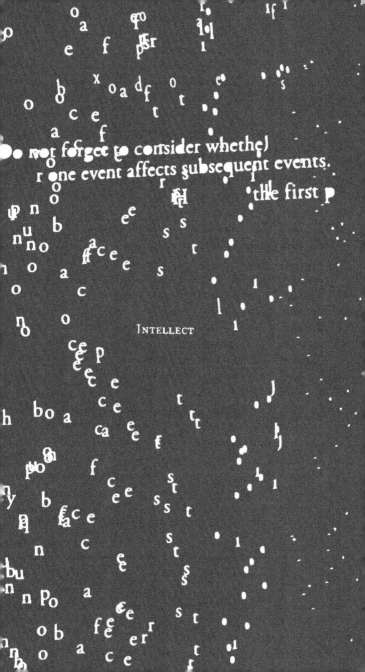

3
2
Nowmultiply.
LATISSIMUS DORSI
OBLIQUUS ABDOMINIS
EXTERNUS
GLUTEUS MEDIUS
GLUTEUS MAXIMUS
TENSOR
FASCIA LATA
FASCIA LATA,
ILIOTIBIAL
TRACT
5
9
1
1

The first roll of a die or flip of a

coin has no effect on any subsequent rolls

s   b   n

However, the first pick of an object does

b   affect subsequent picks if you do not r

Thus, the probability of picking two is

Don't forget to consider whether one event affects subsequent events

or flips However, the first pick of an object does

affect subsequent picks if you do not replace that object. Check whether the object is replaced

back into the scenario in order before the second and subsequent picks.

$$\frac{3}{10} \times \frac{2}{9} = \frac{3}{10}^{1} \times \frac{2}{9}^{1} = \frac{1}{15}$$

Notes
• Performing high, flexion with the feet in dorsiflexion
  works mainly the gastrocnemius
• Performing high flexions with the feet in plantar
  flexion works mainly the hamstring muscle

THE CHAPEL

muffled silence

They do not need the obstetric forceps of the surgeon,

The insignificant is as big to me as any,

(What is less or more than a touch?)

Logic and sermons never convince,

The damp of the night drives deeper into my soul.

(Only what proves itself to each man and woman is so,

Only what nobody denies is so.)

A minute and a drop of me settle my brain,

I believe the soggy clods shall become lovers and lamps,

And a compend of compends is the meat of a man or woman,

And a summit and flower there is the feeling they have for each other,

And they are to branch boundlessly out of that lesson until it becomes omnific,

And until one and all shall delight us, and we them.

I believe a leaf of grass is no less than the journey-work of the stars,

And the pismire is equally perfect, and a grain of sand, and the egg of the wren,

And the tree-toad is a chef-d'œuvre for the highest,

And the running blackberry would adorn the parlors of heaven,

And the narrowest hinge in my hand puts to scorn all machinery,

And the cow crunching with depress'd head surpasses any statue,

And a mouse is miracle enough to stagger sextillions of infidels.

I find I incorporate gneiss, coal, long-threaded moss, fruits, grains, esculent roots,

And am stucco'd with quadrupeds and birds all over,

And have distanced what is behind me for good reasons,

But call any thing back again when I desire it.

poor devils,

measureless power

cearnestness

rising fury,

kerd

d   life · t.

THERE is one mind common to all individua
Of the works of this mind, history is
illustrated by the entire series of days.
nothing less than all his history.
and the limits of nature   Man is
give power to but one
every faculty, every thought, every emotion,
Each law in turn is made by circumstances
p
1 thousand forests is in one acorn,
G

n
m 1 .
d
r
t
w o h
e

l
v h
This human   o   istory,
s
The Sphinx mu t s e   riddle
.
e r
o
w n

If the whole is in one man,
it is all to be explained from indivi
ence.
There is a relation between the hours

This human mind wrote history
The Sphinx must solve her own riddle

ART

GHT BAR

But not by the
souls of the men,
nor by dæmons of
earth or middle
air, but by a
blessed troop of
angelic spirits,
sent down by the
invocation of the
guardian saint.

Like corpses in a charnel:
time and change
Invulnerable nothings
unquenchably the same,

Beware of

cold hopes

these carrion-kites that scream
Back to the burning fountain
and myself the same

wondrous, they are
in respect to the measureless self
his measureless power
But it was time to return to
thy epidemic, man

There is no pennance, much less innocence:
To teach thee, I am naked first; why then
What needst thou **more**

Not enjoyment, and not sorrow
But to act that each to-morrow

"Dust thou art, to dust returnest,"
Was not spoken of the soul.

Amidst the storm they sang,
  And the stars heard, and the sea;

And the heavy night hung dark
    In silence and in fear.

What sought they thus afar?
The wealth of seas? the spoils of war?—
  Bright jewels? our living clay?

And our hearts, though stout
  and brave,
  Convulse us and consume us
          day by day,

Still, like muffled drums, are beating
  Funeral marches to the grave.

Art is long, and Time is fleeting,

perhaps
     on
      our
       shipwrecked
         lives

all sublime
    leaves us
at life's **main**.
sands of **solemn** time:
sands of remind
sands of behind
    perhaps **another**
      life

Be
pleasant!
a Swallow
remind my
whole
Head!
Future,
herb time:
Present And,
be
act
in Past
perspective,
Let
It
sands illusion,
eyes.
world
truly
mountain
looks
far
like
hidden. through
range the
away,
my all
leave but
enough If
lives
strife not
no
behind
was
Trust then make
us
God
bury us
within
o'erhead!
Act, dead
the
sublime,
were
howe'er
living
Footprints
great and
from now
departing

hi

there

a
or
nor
not
men,
But
dæmons
down
the
the
the
of
saint.
of
of
earth
of
but
souls
air,
invocation
by
by
by
blessed
angelic
by
sent
spirits,
middle
guardian

Did your pain feel numb?

Very much

Very much

A little bit

A little bit

Somewhat

Somewhat

Quite a bit

Quite a bit

Did your pain feel
distant and day-long?

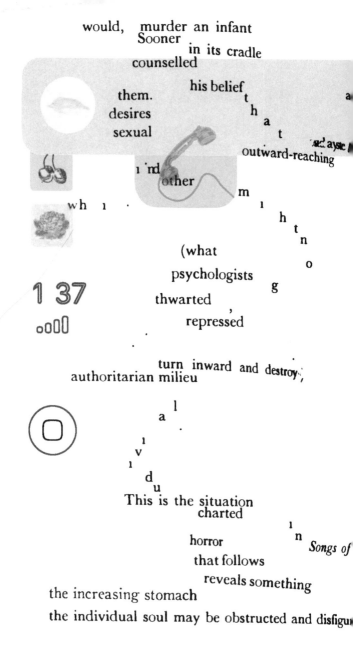

would, murder an infant
Sooner in its cradle
counselled

his belief
them. t
desires h a t
sexual t
outward-reaching

nd
other m i
h
t
wh i n

o
g

(what
psychologists
1 37 thwarted ,
repressed
oOO

.

turn inward and destroy,
authoritarian milieu

l
a
.
i
v
i
d
u
This is the situation
charted

i
horror n *Songs of*
that follows
reveals something
the increasing stomach
the individual soul may be obstructed and disfigur

The Garden of Love

I went   'Chapel',
innocence has been left behind.
And saw what I never had seen:

And tomb-stones where flowers should be:
So I turned to the Garden of Love,
That so many sweet flowers bore,
And 'Thou shalt not' writ over the door;
And I saw it was filled with graves,
And binding with briars my joys & desires
                    were walking their rounds,
And the gates of this Chapel were shut,

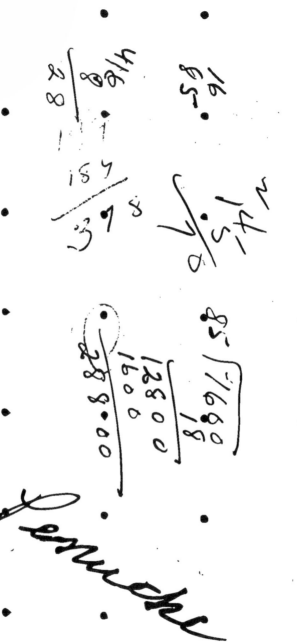

THE POET

the event

you weep

so fine   reasonable

so hard to be observed

wept

Tell me   such a misfortune   full of zeal

it can afford   banish sorrow

laid on an anvil.   followed.

their faith,   These difficulties are common

goodness

by concealment

acquire additional value

worthy

virtuous woman   But you

shapes awaits them.   perilous.

fully

your situation

, they rush

I hope

the folly

this be a poetical fiction

according to the poet,

trial of the cup

regardless of danger,

this subject,

they are glorious and profitable

this be a poetical fiction

perceive in the enemy's wall a breach
        you were so fortunate
        l   f   l l
Soon as the blushing morn his crime betrays:
There is no jewel in the world so valuable
But, self-condemned, and e'en self-punished, lies
                more to say
of the world
           conception,   the goods
      The honor of women
         estimation   self-reproaches
expose her to danger, the consciousness
              glory from above

Consider, then, my friend 'St. Peter, —
reputation among men · more prudent
When most unseen, then most himself he sees,
Shame, grief, remorse, in Peter's breast increase,
And with due horror all his soul surveys.

To wound his soul, when conscious of a fault;
" 'For a great spirit needs no censuring eyes
And dreads no witness like upbraiding Thought,
she cannot rise in value
(What is less or more than a touch?)

possess

g

Do I astonish more

than they?

In me the caresser

of life

how fast I run!

**SACRED
TO THE MEMORY**

fire

,

(K ,

I (

,

1

I A₁

w

) (.

o u

r ʳ

ʳ

e o

v

o c

c e

.

(

s s

I made them hurry

t

every·man did

d

force; h ¹ a load

l I a mild and gentle ·

tapestry and old cloth

with pewter trees, A it

year rising fury,

to examine fire two of

from the rain. hand them

I alacrity, butcher weighing

first bundles pine-trees

this violent fire

dying.

I began to melt

U

`·

Divinity

t
l
h
p
\

l

l

water   r
optional   s
paper   p   t   \g
syrup   g
o   water to
chopped
a   cold
n   consta
o   is   gf
beat
m   until
cold in
a   small
forms   h
Heat   s
point to
o   un hold
and   (
annua and   t
u   and   )
candy
beating
begins   y   e
Combine
constantly mix
occasionally Beat   w
stirring
n   cook,   s
y   dropped
foamy
syrup
(252 degrees).   Add
teaspoonfuls
hold
onto its
hard shape
Hold on

the event

you weep

arranged close together

THE MAGNETIC

A ... indicate ... F

as well as ... the lines ... cross each ... the

closes upon itself

the force has direction

Do I

defunct

to roam

perforating
a pulsing field

moving bodies

so-slightly

media

I am large, I contain multitudes

compared to a man

This

blooming ... in the direction of

the man exerts a force

there is no motion of the house.

becoming the same direction and the

which extend

lines of force

carefully constructed divide between the spread

each other seldom counts for the

but like ... and rubber ... accounts around the poles of a magnet

finding their range

in the metal of the magnet because

They a good conductor

lines of force.

are drawn together   o

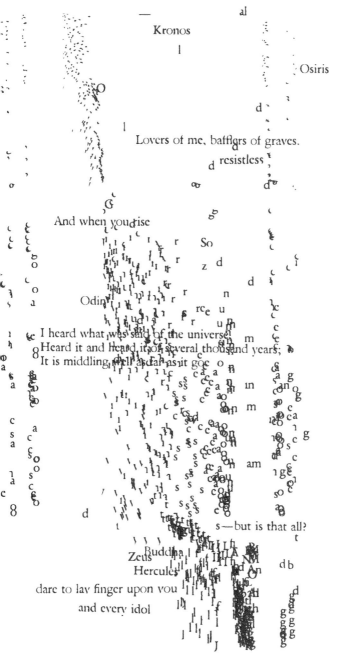

al

Kronos

l

Osiris

d

O

l

Lovers of me, bafflers of graves.

d resistless

G

And when you rise

So

z d

d

Odin

I heard what was said of the universe

Heard it and heard it of several thousand years;

It is middling well as far as it goes

s—but is that all?

Buddha

Zeus

Hercules

db

dare to lay finger upon you

and every idol

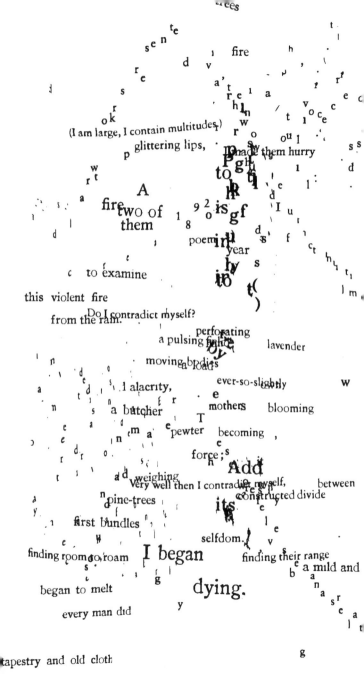

trees

fire

(I am large, I contain multitudes,)

glittering lips,

made them hurry

A
fire two of
them

9 2
1 8 0

is g

poem in
year

to examine

this violent fire

from the rain. Do I contradict myself?

perforating
a pulsing

lavender

moving abroad

1 alacrity,

ever-so-slightly

w

a butcher

mothers

blooming

pewter becoming ,

force;

Add

weighing

Very well then I contradict myself,

between

constructed divide

pine-trees

its

first bundles

selfdom.

finding room to roam

I began

finding their range

a mild and

began to melt

dying.

every man did

tapestry and old cloth

g

POLITICS

left to the
fear of danger

inhabit this temple of the body

for good reasons,

The earth good

and the stars

How and earth perfect are eternal
How perfect all good is perfect the minutest
beautiful perfect, and is just
Genius studies the causal thought, eral are all ober
ponderable fluids perfect
they have
men diving Wh th e v y et pass on
Nothing is
I think now that everything
The trees have rooted in the ground divine weeds
I swear I think there is nothing but immortality the bruteness
cause and effect
Genius detects
That the exquisite scheme is for
for it, and the coherring is
And all preparation is for it am identity
and materials are all to

its growth,
all events pre friendly and sacred
the philosophe
m
Slowly and surely last night's profitable
cidents of appearance poet makes twenty fables
and surely
which neglects surface TO THINK OF TIME

ts surf:
an eternal soul!

the clearer vision of causes

and surrounded as we are by this

they fall by infinite diameters.

I did it

it is true

What is less
than a touch
nobody denies?
Only what
or more
is so.

How would were you
when this happened?

At the time of the event did
you believe that you or someone
else could be killed □ YES □ NO
seriously *harmed*?

At the time of the event did
you experience feelings so *intense*
helplessness fear □ YES □ NO
horror?

How much has this affected
your life in the past year?

□ 1   □ 2   □ 3 □ 4 □ 5
not at all somewhat extremely

unconditio

And

under

the

stars

they

shall

be

murderers,

liars

th

a

t

past

and

present

is

now

under

the

law

are

F

o

r

that

I

dream'd

enough

l perdition

se roi usyl **ha mre d** ?

ngota.ta.lksoorer-ex-tmre-est

MANNERS

Upborne and surrounded
bruteness and toughness
cause and effect
always and never the same.

good enough for a carcass
when they seest me

I m bouncing
between impermanent
things

ripping strips
of sheets and
ripping me

R
Spanis
and flesh

y

tho

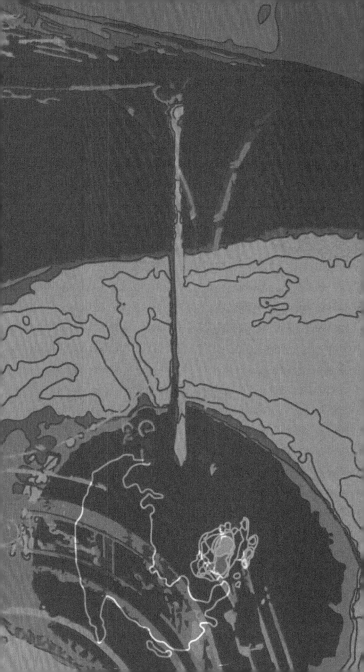

This human mind

wrote history

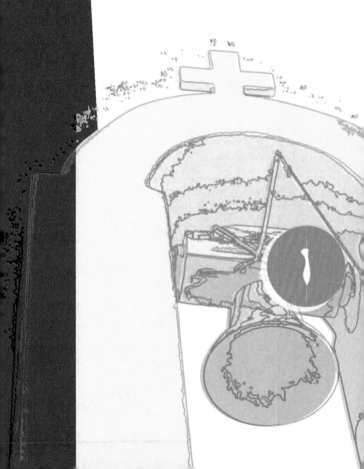

the eternal unity.

Drape me

over the edge

pincher claw

crusher claw

beware

beware

assemble

the army

This town

This human mind wrote history
The Sphinx must solve her own riddle
.

why did your pain feel tender?

CHARACTER

I assume a steady,
common-sense exterior

**But what am I
questioning?**

Don't I know that
the stars don't move?

war

I am questioning
the universal manifesta-
tion of God to all the world
with all those misty blurs.

La morte della
della
Connessione

all the facts of history preëxist

regardless of danger;

Let the dead Past bury its dead!

the lie folded already in

our destined end or way.

whole from my perspective
   an illusion
            ☐ YES   ☐ NO

We can make our lives sublime,
   extremely   ☐ YES   ☐ NO

"Dust thou art, to dust returnest,"
            ☐ YES   ☐ NO

there were no clouds
            ☐ YES   ☐ NO

'Shame, grief, remorse,
            ☐ YES   ☐ NO

Is our destined end or way
            ☐ YES   ☐ NO

Trust
            ☐ 4   ☐ 5

Not enjoyment, and not sorrow

            ☐ YES   ☐ NO

      Was not spoken
            ☐ YES   ☐ NO
   no Future, howe'er pleasant!
            ☐ YES   ☐ NO

         ☐ 4   ☐ 5
                    extremely

GIFTS

belief

no less
than the
journey-work of
the stars,

Art is long, and Time is fleeting,

agnus dei

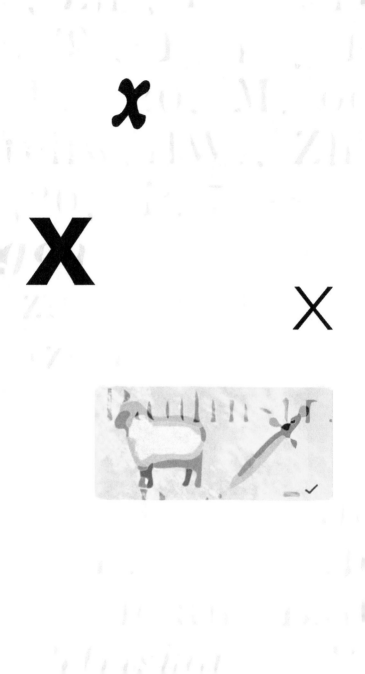

Adhae

pavim

anima

mea

sit

ento

EXPERIENCE

Turn SMS notifications off?

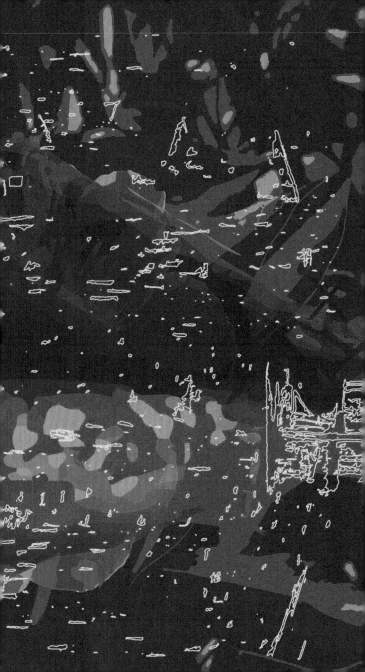

A D   2 is

1 is Suff   2 is N O T Suff

~~DCL~~

1 is S   O   T   S   ff

is
is NOT Suff

N O T Suff

2 is Suff

2 is

N O T Suff

Location services have ~~have~~ been turned off

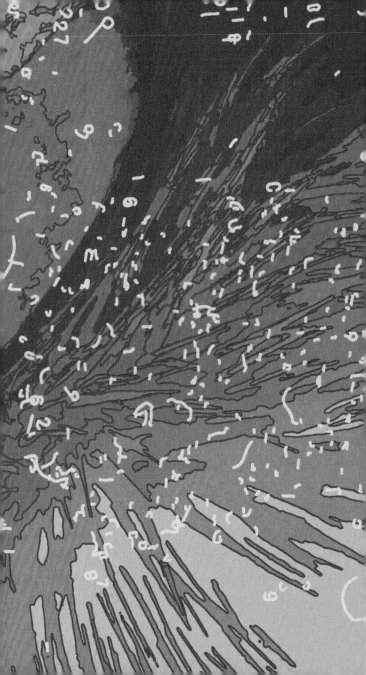

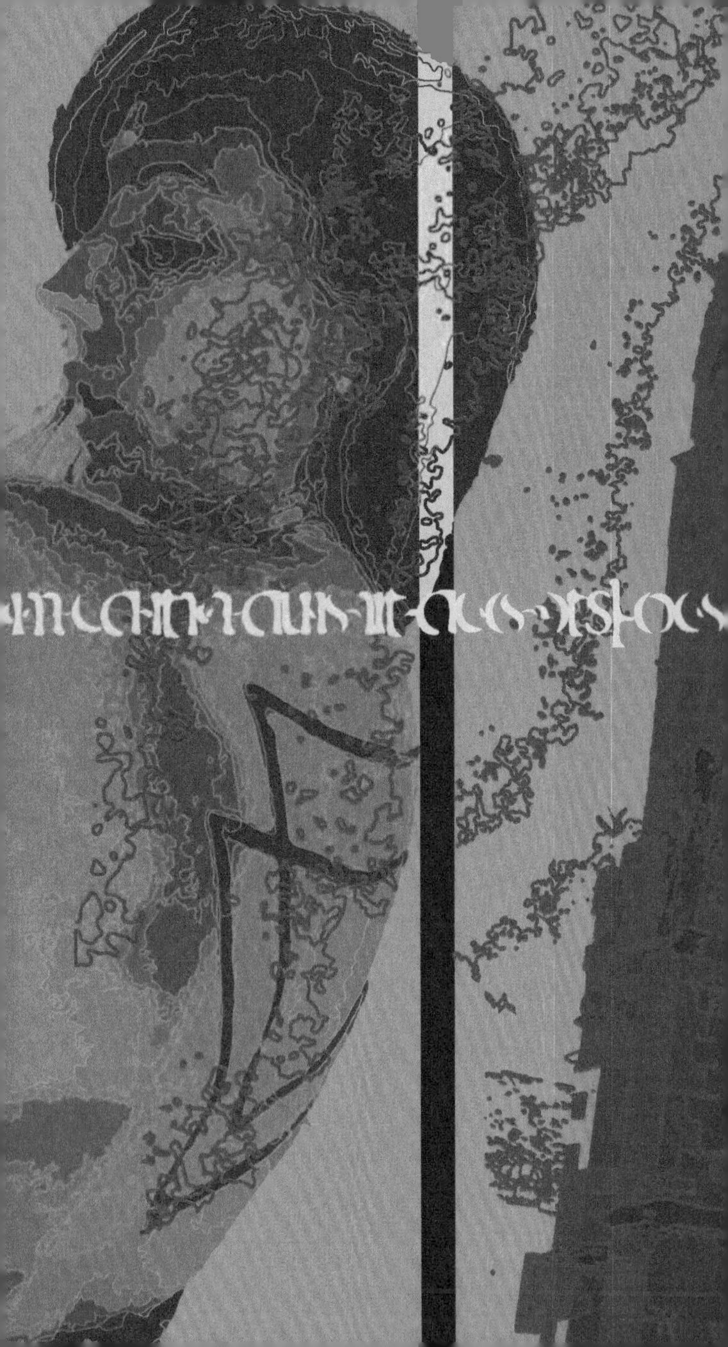

you see
my heart,
you know
my de-
sires

**possess
all I am**

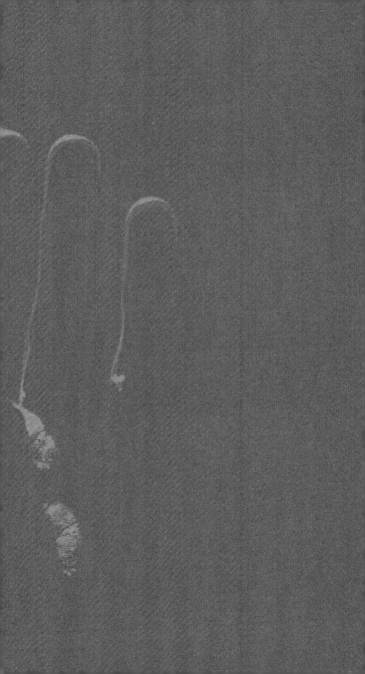

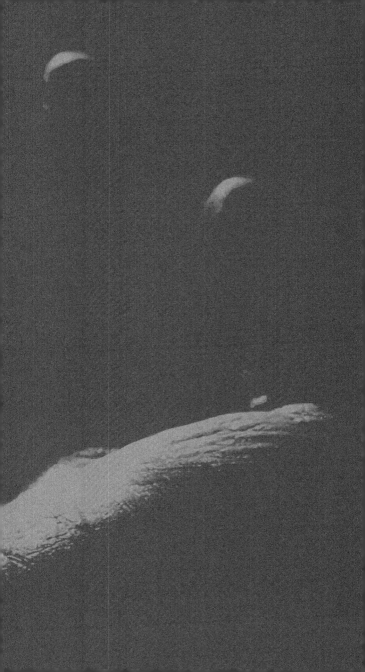

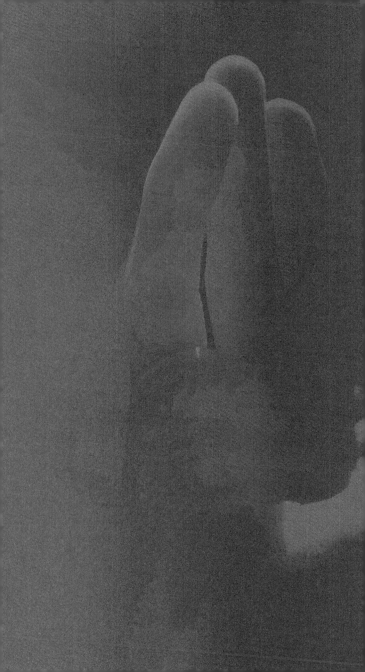

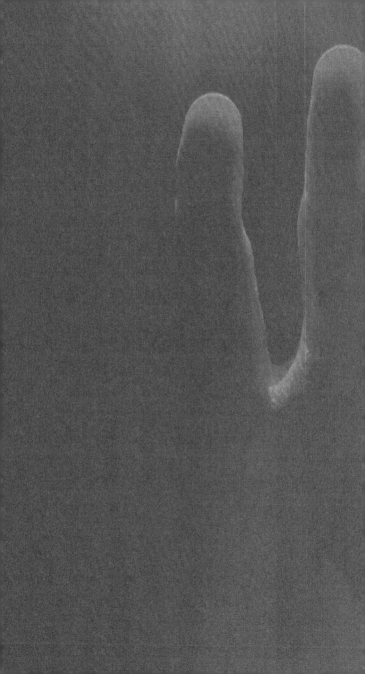

why did your pain feel tender?

(What is less or more than a touch?)

Only what nobody denies is so.

nobody denies

I believe

I believe

I believe

I believe a leaf

I believe

the stars,

I believe

the journey-

I believe   the   work

I believe   no less

I believe a leaf of grass

I believe I believe I b

I believe

believe I believe

I believe

I believe I believe

I believe

I believe

I believe I

I believe

I believe I believe

I believe

I believe

I believe

I believe

. . . . .

I believe

I believe

I believe I believe

I I I I I I Ibe

believe

c c c c c c

I believe

I believe I believe

b b b b b b b

I I I I

I I I

I believe

I believe I believe

I believe I believe

I believe

I believe

I believe I believe

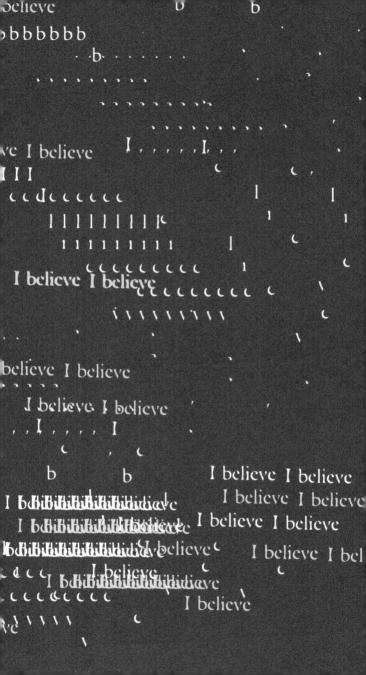

NATURE

caterpillar

the eye is fastened on the life

toughness of matter

the genus

the grub
Nature is a mutable

obeying its law

appearance.

These difficulties are common
the womb of things

soft and fluid as a cloud

goodness

acquire additional value
of time

w

churches.
sees the rays parting

psychosis of nature
by concealment

heir faith

worthy
virtuous woman
perilous,

But you

all his masks.

Each law in turn is made by circumstances

a leaf of grass

the stars

palm crown

This is the situation
charted

horror
that follows
reveals something
in the living Present,

They do not know how immortal,
but I know.

I went
And saw what I never had seen:
Innocence left behind

an

I contradict myself.

constructed divide

o k

I contain multitudes.

perforating   lips,

moving bodies

ever-so-slightly

between

lavender

a pulsing field   mother

blooming

finding range

becoming

finding room to roam

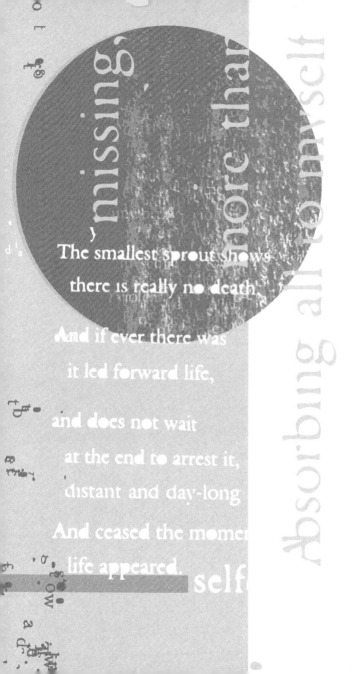

missing,

more than

Absorbing all to myself

The smallest sprout shows
there is really no death.
And if ever there was
it led forward life,

and does not wait
at the end to arrest it,
distant and day-long
And ceased the momer
life appeared.

self

It seems to me more
than myself
missing,

You find yourself at the end of Saint Agatha Mother Redeemer, a work of experimental poetry.

This is a book about proximity. I write this with the hope that you have found distance between yourself and the person or persons who harmed you, and between the memories that remain and your life now.

No anti-rape device exists.
We have each other and
we have the possibility
of building new systems
of care and transforming
justice.

M. Saith Gole

saint agatha
mother
redeemer

michèle saint-michel

Michèle Saint-Michel—born in northwest Missouri, the daughter of a farmer's daughter and a railroad-man's son—was raised by a salesman and a librarian. She spent much of her childhood barefoot, baking mud pies and traipsing through the woods. She wrote and danced and talked quite a lot before she moved to the mountains. After some time in the snow and ancient shorelines, she grew tired of the landscape, so she set off to see more of the
w   o   r   l   d   .

Saint-Michel is an intermedia artist, experimental filmmaker, and poet. She wrote this book over several years after surviving a series of traumatic experiences. The events were impossible to talk about for a long time. By borrowing the words of other poets and writers, she found a way—finally—to begin to speak about what
h   a   p   p   e   n   e   d   .
It   remains   difficult   to   talk   about.

Also from Michèle Saint-Michel, look for

Grief is an Origami Swan

Liner Notes for Getting Out Without Catching Fire

Printed in Great Britain
by Amazon